THE GROUP APPROACH TO DRAMA

Pupils' Book One

THE GROUP APPROACH TO DRAMA

This series consists of:

Pupils' Book One

Pupils' Book Two

Pupils' Book Three

Pupils' Book Four

Teacher's Book

THE GROUP APPROACH TO DRAMA

Pupils' Book One

D. E. Adland

MASTER IN CHARGE OF DRAMA
CORNER HALL SECONDARY SCHOOL, HEMEL HEMPSTEAD

Illustrated by Charles Keeping

LONGMAN

LONGMAN GROUP LIMITED
LONDON
*Associated companies, branches and representatives
throughout the world*

*First published 1964
Sixth impression 1968
Eighth impression 1969
Ninth impression 1969*

SBN 582 21933 7

Acknowledgments

We are grateful to the following for permission to use copyright material:
J.M. Dent & Sons Ltd for 'St. George and the Dragon' from Appendix A
of *Everyman and other Interludes,* and the Public Trustee and the Society of
Authors for material from *Androcles and the Lion* by Bernard Shaw.

PRINTED IN HONG KONG
BY DAI NIPPON PRINTING CO (INTERNATIONAL) LTD

CONTENTS

PART I

Part Two of this book, begins on p. 25

PAIR PLAYS

Plays for Two Actors

Read this first

In the first part of this book there are six 'Pair' Plays.

All the plays can be given by two actors.

The Plays can be acted without words (as a Mime).

Or you can make up your own words (as an Improvisation).

There are also two 'Pair' Plays giving words which you can use in your own way or learn.

You can make up your own 'Pair' Plays and act them.

NOW
Find a partner.
Choose a play.
Read it through.
Cast the parts.
Decide on Mime or Speaking.
Act it.

Then

Think of a title.
Make up a 'Pair' Play of your own.

THE COIN

A Play for Two

People

Two boys, PETE and JOHN.

Place

A street.

Plan of Action

  1. Walking home, hands in pockets, kicking stones.

  2. Pete kicks, hears a coin, and picks it up.

  3. John rushes over and looks at the coin.

  4. They look at the coin, wonder what to do with it.

  5. They search for other coins...

  6. ... but they do not find any.

  7. They look through the sweetshop window, point out different sweets.

  8. They argue about what to buy...

  9. ... so they toss the coin—and it spins away.

10. They search frantically.

11. They give up and walk on, hands in pockets, kicking stones.

Feeling

Miserable, 'fed-up'.

Surprised, pleased.

Curious, interested.

Both delighted.

Excited, hopeful.

A little disappointed.

Eager, happy.

Anxious, cross.

Alarmed, fearful.

Becoming more and more worried.

Miserable, 'fed-up'.

Now make up a play like this, where two boys find something—a ring, a dog-collar, a brooch...whatever you like.

2

Planning The Play

THE OLD MISER

A Play for Two

How do we know he is a miser?
He carefully counts his money.

How do we know he is old?
He walks slowly, his back is bent, his hands shake and he can't see very well.

What happens?
Someone comes in—and robs him.

What does the robber do?
He creeps up behind the old miser, and suddenly knocks him down.

Now what?
The robber snatches up the money-box and runs out.

Is that the end?
It could be. Or the police might catch the robber.

Now find a partner and act The Old Miser.
One is the Miser, the other is the Robber.
After the first go, change over parts.
Try to do it silently, without any words, as a Mime.
Then try it with words, making them up as you go along, as an improvisation.
Now get someone to play the policeman and do the whole play.

3

Building up the Play

THE OLD MISER

A Play for Five

How many people are there so far?
There's the old miser, the robber and the policeman.

How can we make the play bigger?
Put in some more people—perhaps two more.

Who could they be?
Anyone—friends, neighbours, relatives, the postman, the milkman, a salesman.

What could they do?
They could call on the miser and talk about different things.

As he's a miser what would they talk about?
Money. They want to be paid or they want to borrow some.

What would the old miser do?
He wouldn't give them any. He would push them out and slam the door.

And then his money is stolen.
Yes. It serves him right because he wouldn't help anyone.

Supposing all those he wouldn't help catch the robber and return the money?
He would be very pleased because he loves money. Then he might be sorry for the way he had behaved and help them after all.

Now that this play has been built up you need five actors to play the parts.

4

MISER   ROBBER   POLICEMAN   A CALLER   ANOTHER
CALLER

Talk over the play.
Decide who the 'callers' are to be.
Decide how the robber is to be caught.
Cast the parts.
Act the play in your own way.

After Acting

When you have acted this play in your own way, look at the
Complete Play of *The Old Miser* on the next page.
Cast the parts again and act this Complete Play.

The Complete Play

THE OLD MISER

ALL the parts can be played by two actors but you can have three or four or five.

People

OLD MISER

THE ROBBER

A NEIGHBOUR, who is hard-up ⎫

A TRAMP   ⎬ *One actor can play all these parts*

POLICEMAN   ⎭

Place

Miser's house; A street.

Plan of Action

1. The miser sits at his desk. He opens a small box with a tiny key which he has trouble in finding. He slowly counts the coins inside, taking them out one by one.
2. One coin is missing! Becoming more and more frantic, he searches everywhere until he finds it.
3. Knock at the door. He replaces the coins, counting as he does so, and relocks the box. He unlocks the door.
4. A neighbour asks the miser to lend him a pound till the end of the week. The miser grumpily refuses to help him and pushes him out.
5. A tramp begs for food—and he is willing to work for it. The miser laughs at him and drives him away.
6. A robber creeps very quietly behind the miser, knocks him over the head and runs out with his money-box.
7. *If there are only two of you act it this way:*
   The robber now plays the part of the neighbour. He

returns the miser's money, explaining that he and the tramp caught him running out with it. The police have got him now.

If you have a group of five act it this way:

The robber is seen by the neighbour who tries to stop him. Then the tramp joins in. Finally, the police arrive and arrest the robber.

8. The miser is delighted with the return of his money—and gratefully rewards both the tramp and the neighbour.

Another 'Miser' Play

There is a play about a miser called SCROOGE on p. 46. It is called *Happy Christmas!*

THE ARMCHAIR

A Play for Six

All the parts can be played by two actors but you can have three or four or five or six.

People

Two boys, TED and JOE
Ted's GRANDFATHER
BUTCHER
SHOPKEEPER
MANAGER OF FIREWORKS FACTORY

} *As a 'Pair'
Play Ted and
Joe can play all
the parts*

Place

Ted's back garden
Butcher's shop

Newsagent's shop
Fireworks factory

Ted's back garden

Plan of Action

1. While building a bonfire, the two boys decide to get the old armchair the dog sleeps on. They get it and sit the 'guy' in it. (*You could have one of your group playing the part of the 'guy' for this scene.*)

2. Ted goes off for a drink of water. Grandfather comes out shouting angrily (*he is played by Ted if there are only two of you*), and pulls the armchair off the bonfire. The chair falls and splits and money rolls out.

3. GRANDFATHER: Don't bother about the chair. Now I can buy Rover a new one. Here's some money for fireworks.

4. Grandfather goes off to buy a new armchair. Ted comes back and Joe tells him about the money. They are both delighted and decide to hold a big bonfire party.

5. Butcher's shop. (*Joe can play the Butcher.*) Ted buys a huge chicken, pies, sausages and legs of ham.

6. Newsagent's shop. (*Ted can play the Shopkeeper.*) Joe buys two pounds' worth of fireworks.   But Joe wants a really big firework.
7. Fireworks factory.   Joe sees the Manager and buys an enormous rocket for five pounds. (*Ted plays the Manager.*)
8. Garden. The boys meet and show each other what they have bought. They get the party ready and finally set off the giant rocket.

About this Play

This 'Pair' Play—a play with lots of people and scenes acted by only two—was written down by two First Year pupils after they had acted it.

NOW

Make up your own 'Pair' Play.
Get a partner and choose a title.

> FOOTPRINTS IN THE SAND
> THE STOLEN SPUDS
> THE SCIENTIST'S GREAT DISCOVERY
> TIME-BOMB
> THE NEW DUST-BIN
> THE FRIGHTENED SOLDIER

You can have as many scenes as you like.
You can have as many people as you like—as long as there are only two on at a time.

THE BOX
A Play for Two

Get a friend as a partner.
Make up a play called The Box.

What kind of people are you?
Anxious, excitable, gloomy, quick-tempered? Try to play
your parts as *different* people.

Where do you find the box?

On the beach	In an attic
In an old house	On the ledge of a cliff
Down a hole or cave	In the boot of a car

In fact, anywhere you like.

How do you find it?
Accidentally
   —*while playing a game.*
   —*while looking for something else.*
   —*by falling over it, or onto it.*
   —*while exploring a place.*
On purpose
   —*because it has been lost, or stolen.*
   —*searching for treasure.*
   —*because you saw it there, or being put there.*

What sort of box is it?
Is it small or large...wood, metal or cardboard...strong
with locks...fragile, easily opened?

What's in the box?
Something valuable—*like jewels or money*—is what everybody
would expect.
Why not—
Something disappointing—*like stones or paper or rags.*

Something surprising — *like antique pistols or a skeleton.*
Something dangerous — *like a time-bomb or gunpowder.*
Something funny — *like a wig, a string of sausages, rotten eggs,
an old tramp asleep (big box!)*

What do you do with what you find?

Depends what it is. You might keep it, use it, play with it,
get hurt by it, eat it, take it to the police or just throw it away.
It's up to you.

THE BOX

A Scripted Play for Two

Here is the first scene of a 'Box' play written by a fourth year pupil. You can learn the parts and act it or you can just take the idea and use your own words.

People

WURZEL, a farm labourer
GILES, a farmer

Place:

A field.

Wurzel is sitting, eating.

WURZEL [*thinking aloud*]: Ah, it be a lovely day to-day, wi' all the old sun shinin' over th' meadow and the cuckoo cuckooing all over the place. [*He takes a few bites at his sandwich.*] 'Ullo—what be this a-comin' across me field? [*He chews slowly.*] Ah, it be Farmer Giles in one o' they new-fangled fings called tractors....'Ullo, Jack! 'Ow be ee this fine day?

GILES: All right, thanks Wurzel. I got summat to tell ee.

WURZEL: What?

GILES: Aunt Flossie's died.

WURZEL [*jumping up*]: No!

GILES: Yes, and she left twenty thousand pounds to the person 'oo finds 'er Will.

WURZEL: There'll be a reg'lar ol' treasure hunt, won't there!

GILES: Ay, there will be at that...Wal, I must be goin'. [*Goes.*]

WURZEL: Cheerio...[*He sits down, then leaps up quickly.*] Aaaahh! They dang thistles is everywhere! I'll cut the bloomin' fings down! [*He hacks furiously with a stick or sickle*]. Take that! and that! and that!...Oh, me hand! 'Ullo, what be this?...A liddle box—I wonder what's in it? I'll bop it one wi' me spade. [*He strikes the box and it breaks.*] There be a liddle piece o' paper in it. [*He looks at it, puzzled.*] Hmph! I can't read writin' when it's writ... Ah, I know—I'll go an' ask Farmer Giles. He can read an' write an' say the alphabet backwards. [*He starts to go but stops short.*] No need, 'ere ee comes now. I wonder what ee wants. [*Shouts.*] 'Ullo, Jack, you're just the chappie I was comin' t'see.

GILES: Sorry to bother you agin, but I think I left me pipe somewheres—ah, there she is [*picks it up*]. What do ee want me for?

WURZEL: To read this.

GILES: Give 'un 'ere then [*takes paper*]. Ah, it's in rhyme—
[*reads*] Who ever finds this Will
   His pockets with money shall fill,
   With twenty thousand pounds or more
   When he sees my solicitor.
Signed Aunt Flo...there!

WURZEL: It's Aunt Flossie's Will! [*He dances around shouting.*] I'll be a wealthy millionaire, whoopee, whahoo!!

GILES [*catching him by the arm*]: All right, all right. Calm down.

WURZEL: Oh, yes...'Oo be 'er solicitor?

GILES: It says where to find him on the back. It says—Silas Snob, 24 Plushbeam Road, Upshire. That don't be far from 'ere. Come on. [*They go off.*]

Can you make up a second scene for this play?
What happens when Giles and Wurzel meet Silas Snob?

GUITAR CRAZY!

A Play for Five

All the parts can be played by two actors but you can have three or four or five.

People

RONNIE

HIS DAD

OLD MAN, owner of Music Shop

POSTMAN

JEWELLER, a smart young man

} *One actor can play all these parts*

Place

Home.

Music Shop.

Street.

Jeweller's Shop.

Music Shop.

Plan of Action

1. It's Ronnie's birthday, but Dad has forgotten to get him a present. He is disappointed until Dad gives him ten shillings. He decides to buy a guitar.
2. Music shop. The guitars are too expensive. Finally the old man offers him a violin for ten shillings. Ronnie isn't very keen—but the old man persuades him. He'll even teach him to play it.
3. Street. Ronnie bumps into a postman delivering letters. Letters scatter everywhere—and the violin breaks. They are both angry and upset. Then Ronnie finds a bag of old gold coins inside the broken violin.
4. Jeweller's shop. Happily, Ronnie sells the coins, explaining how he got them.
5. Music shop. Ronnie runs in—and buys the best guitar in the shop!

Make up your own 'Pair' Plays

Choose one of these titles:

THE KNIFE	THE ANTIQUE PISTOLS
THE KEY	THE FROG
THE OLD BOOT	THE TELEGRAM
THE WALLET	THE PENNY 'BANGER'
THE RING	THE BROKEN WINDOW

These are plays about 'things'.
You have already seen four plays about 'things' in this book:

THE COIN

THE BOX

THE ARMCHAIR

GUITAR CRAZY!

These will help your own play-making. And of course you can make up your own titles for your plays.

ST. GEORGE AND THE DRAGON

A Cornish Christmas Play for Five

People

Saint George	The Doctor
The Dragon	Turkish Knight
Father Christmas	

FATHER CHRISTMAS: Here come I, old Father Christmas,
                Welcome, or welcome not,
                I hope old Father Christmas,
                Will never be forgot.
    I am not come here to laugh or to jeer,
    But for a pocketful of money, and a skinful of beer.

SAINT GEORGE: Here come I, St. George, from Britain did
                I spring,
                I'll fight the dragon bold, my wonders to begin.
                I'll clip his wings, he shall not fly;
                I'll cut him down, or else I die.

DRAGON: Who's he that seeks the Dragon's blood,
                And calls so angry, and so loud?
                That English dog, will he before me stand?
                I'll cut him down with my courageous hand.

[*St. George and the Dragon fight, and the Dragon is killed*]

FATHER CHRISTMAS: Is there a doctor to be found
                All ready, near at hand,
                To cure a deep and deadly wound,
                And make the champion stand?

DOCTOR: Oh yes! there is a doctor to be found
                All ready, near at hand,
                To cure a deep and deadly wound,
                And make the champion stand.

FATHER CHRISTMAS: What can you cure?

DOCTOR: All sorts of diseases,
  Whatever you pleases.

FATHER CHRISTMAS: What is your fee?

DOCTOR: Fifteen pound, it is my fee,
  The money to lay down.
  But, as 'tis such a rogue as thee,
  I cure for ten pound.
  I carry a little bottle of alicumpane;
  Here Jack, take a little of my flip flop,
  Pour it down thy tip top;
  Rise up and fight again.

[*The Doctor performs his cure, the fight is renewed, and the Dragon is killed again*]

SAINT GEORGE: Where is the man, that now will me defy?
  I'll cut his giblets full of holes, and make his buttons fly.

TURKISH KNIGHT: Here come I, the Turkish Knight,
  Come from the Turkish land to fight.
  I'll fight Saint George, who is my foe,
  I'll make him yield before I go.

SAINT GEORGE: Where is the Turk, that will before me stand?
  I'll cut him down with my courageous hand.

[*They fight, the Knight is overcome, and falls on one knee.*]

TURKISH KNIGHT: Oh! pardon me, Saint George, pardon of thee I crave,
  Oh! pardon me this night, and I will be thy slave.

SAINT GEORGE: No pardon shalt thou have, while I have foot to stand,
  So rise thee up again, and fight out sword in hand.

[*They fight again, and the Knight is killed. Father Christmas calls for the Doctor with the same words as before, and the cure is performed with the words,* I carry a little bottle. . . .]

FATHER CHRISTMAS: Now, ladies and gentlemen, your
      sport is most ended,
    So prepare for the hat, which is highly commended.
    The hat it would speak, if it had but a tongue;
    Come throw in your money, and think it no wrong.

THE MAN OF THE ISLAND

A Play for Two

People

JIM HAWKINS, a boy
BEN GUNN, a marooned sailor

Place

Treasure Island.

Plan of Action

1. Jim runs in, terrified. He has just seen Long John Silver
   kill another pirate. Now he rushes away, afraid of pursuit.
2. A sudden noise makes him stop sharply. He sees a strange
   figure leap for cover behind the trunk of a pine.
3. Jim decides to go back, but the figure begins to circle
   round him, springing from cover to cover.
4. Jim remembers his pistol—and starts to walk boldly towards the man of the island. The man steps out to meet
   Jim, hesitates, draws back, comes forward again and finally
   throws himself on his knees, holding out his hands.
5. JIM: Who are you?
   BEN: Ben Gunn. I'm poor Ben Gunn, I am; and I haven't
       spoke with a Christian these three years.
   JIM: Three years! Were you shipwrecked?
   BEN: Nay, mate—marooned. Marooned three years

agone, and lived on goats since then, and berries, and oysters. But, mate, my heart is sore for Christian diet. You mightn't happen to have a piece of cheese about you, now? No? Well, many's the long night I've dreamed of cheese—toasted, mostly—and woke up again, and here I were.

JIM: If ever I get aboard again, you shall have cheese by the stone.

BEN: If ever you get aboard again, says you? Why, now, who's to hinder you?

JIM: Not you, I know.

BEN: And right you was. Now what do you call yourself?

JIM: Jim.

BEN: Jim...Jim...Well, now, Jim, I've lived that rough as you'd be ashamed to hear of. Now, for instance, you wouldn't think I had a pious mother—to look at me?

JIM: Well, no, not in particular.

BEN: Ah, well, but I had—re-markable pious. And I was a civil, pious boy, and could rattle off The Lord's Prayer that fast, as you couldn't tell one word from another. And, Jim [*lowers voice to a whisper*], I'm rich!

JIM: [starting to laugh] Rich—you?

BEN: Rich! rich! I says. And I'll tell you what—I'll make a man of you, Jim. Ah, Jim, you'll bless your stars, you will, that you was the first that found me! [*A cannon booms*]. Hi! what's that?

JIM: They have begun to fight! Follow me. [*They go.*]

Can you make up a second scene for this play? Jim and Ben watch the fight, and then...

ANDROCLES AND THE LION

A Comedy for Three

*When you read this play you will find that some of the original words
of the play,* Androcles and the Lion *by Bernard Shaw, are given,
as well as the Actions.*

*You don't have to use these words. They are there to help you in acting
the scene. You can still make up your own. You* must *make up your
own for some parts of the play.*

*After you have acted the scene with your own words, read the words
again, especially those for Actions 12 and 13. Now when you act
again you will find that you use some of the original words—even
without learning them.*

*Finally you can try learning the words. This won't be difficult when
you have played through the scene once or twice in your own way.*

*And, of course, you could do the whole scene by getting a copy of the
original play on which this scene is based.*

People

ANDROCLES, a small, thin man. Poorly dressed, tired,
hungry.

MEGAERA, a big, well-fed, well-clothed woman, his wife.

A LION

Place

A jungle path near Rome, in Roman times.

Plan of Action

1. A lion's roar—sad, suffering—is heard. The lion limps
   from the jungle, holding up its right forepaw in which a
   huge thorn sticks.

2. The lion sits down and looks at the thorn. He licks it.
   He shakes it. He tries to extract it by scraping it along
   the ground, and hurts himself more.

3. He licks it again and limps painfully off the path and lies down under the trees, exhausted with pain. He goes to sleep.

4. Androcles and his wife Meg come along the path. He carries a huge bundle while Meg has a stout stick to help her along. Suddenly she throws down her stick.

    MEG: I won't go another step.

    AND: Oh, not again, dear. What's the good of stopping every two miles and saying you won't go another step ? We must get to the next village before night. There are wild beasts in this wood: lions, they say.

    MEG: I don't believe a word of it. We haven't seen a single lion yet.

    AND: Well, dear, do you want to see one ?

    MEG [*tearing the bundle from his back*]: You cruel brute, you don't care how tired I am, or what becomes of me [*she throws the bundle on the ground*]: always thinking of yourself. Self! self! self! always yourself! [*She sits down on the bundle.*]

5. Androcles kindly tries to persuade her to come along. Meg sharply tells him off for selling up their home, and for becoming a Christian, for leading her into danger, and for loving animals more than his own wife.

6. At last she gets up, determined to go back home. Androcles bars the way. She rushes off the other way into the jungle...and nearly falls over the sleeping lion !

7. She totters back and collapses into the arms of Androcles, who, crushed by her weight, falls on his bundle.

8. He slaps her hands anxiously and raises her head. She points in the direction of the lion. Androcles steals forward cautiously. Meg totters after him, begging him to come back.

9. Androcles sees the lion and falls back on his wife who falls onto the bundle. They lie staring in horror at one another. The lion groans.

10. MEG: Take me away, Andy. Save me.

    AND: Meggy: there's one chance for you. It'll take him pretty nigh twenty minutes to eat me (I'm rather stringy and tough) and you can escape in less time than that.

    MEG: Oh, don't talk about eating.

11. The lion rises with a great groan and limps towards them. Meg faints.

12. Androcles shakes with fear but keeps between the lion and Meg. Then he notices the thorn. His love for animals overcomes his fear and, with great care and patience, he removes the thorn.

13. The lion thanks him by licking his face and putting his paws round him. Androcles puts his arms round the lion and they waltz off into the jungle. Meg wakes, sees them dancing off and chases after them calling Androcles a coward.

This is how the author of this scene put these two actions into words.

AND: Don't you come near my wife, do you hear?

    [*The lion groans. Andy can hardly stand for trembling.*]

Meggy: run. Run for your life. If I take my eye off him, it's all up.

    [*The lion holds up its wounded paw and flaps it before Androcles.*] Oh, he's lame, poor old chap! He's got a thorn in his paw. A frightfully big thorn. [*Full of sympathy*] Oh, poor old man! Did um get an awful thorn into um's tootsums wootsums? Has it made um too sick to eat a nice little Christian man for um's breakfast? Oh, a nice little Christian man will get um's thorn out for um; and then um shall eat the nice Christian man and the nice Christian man's nice big tender wifey pifey.

[*The lion responds by moans of self-pity.*]

Yes, yes, yes, yes, yes. Now, now [*taking the paw in his hand*], um is not to bite and not to scratch, not even if it hurts a very very little. Now make velvet paws. That's right. [*He pulls gingerly at the thorn. The lion, with an angry yell of pain, jerks back his paw so abruptly that Androcles is thrown on his back.*] Steadee! Oh, did the nasty cruel little Christian man hurt the sore paw? [*The lion nods.*] Well, one more little pull and it will be all over. Just one little little, leetle pull; and then um will live happily ever after. [*He gives the thorn another pull. The lion roars and snaps his jaws with a terrifying clash.*] Oh, mustn't frighten um's good kind doctor, um's affectionate nursey. That didn't hurt at all: not a bit. Just one more. Just to shew how the brave big lion can bear pain, not like the little crybaby Christian man. Oopsh! [*The thorn comes out. The lion yells with pain, and shakes his paw wildly.*]

That's it! [*Holding up the thorn.*] Now it's out. Now lick um's paw to take away the nasty inflammation. See? [*He licks his own hand. The lion nods intelligently and licks his paw industriously.*] Clever little liony-piony! Understand um's dear old friend Andy Wandy. [*The lion licks his face.*] Yes, kissums Andy Wandy.

[*The lion, wagging his tail violently, rises on his hind legs, and embraces Androcles, who makes a wry face and cries*] Velvet paws! Velvet paws! [*The lion draws in his claws.*] That's right. [*He embraces the lion who takes his tail in one paw, places the other on Androcles's waist, and they waltz round and round and finally away through the jungle.*]

MEG [*who has recovered from her faint*]: Oh, you coward, you haven't danced with me for years; and now you go off dancing with a great brute beast that you haven't known for ten minutes and that wants to eat your own wife. Coward! Coward! Coward!

[*She chases off after them.*]

PART II

*All of these plays can be acted by a Group of five or more, with the
exception of some of the scenes in the last three plays. These exceptions
are noted in the text.*

THE GROUP LEADER

The Group Leader has several important jobs to do. If he does them well there will be no muddle over parts and the play will be successful. But he can't do everything by himself. Everyone in the Group must help him.

These are the things the Leader does:

The Group Leader

1. Keeps charge of the Leader's Book.
2. Writes down the parts everyone has in each play.
3. Changes the parts round so that everyone does a big part and a small one, a difficult part and an easy one.
4. Makes sure that everyone knows what they have to do.
5. Sees that everyone gets a fair chance to make suggestions about the play while it can still be changed.
6. Helps the group to decide which is the best way to do the play or scene or Action.
7. Appoints members to be in charge of anything that's needed—like props or costumes or sets.
8. Talks over the play with his group to improve it after rehearsal or performance.
9. Has the final say about who is to take the parts and who is to do the various jobs.

SPRINGBOARD

Group Leader

Read this with your Group so that when you see the word 'Springboard' you will know what to do.

SPRINGBOARD is for the Group Leader and his Group.

SPRINGBOARD comes at the end of each play in Part Two.

SPRINGBOARD shows you how your Group can build up the plays in your own way.

SPRINGBOARD gives you ideas for plays of your own.

SPRINGBOARD gives points for the Group to talk over.

'Springboard' is, in fact, a starting-off or jumping-off point for the Group's own ideas.

THE COALMINE

A story of a disaster

People

LEADER OF THE COALMINE GANG
COALMINERS
RESCUE TEAM

Place

A narrow, ill-lit coal-face.

Plan of Action

1. The miners come on shift with tools, power drill and waggon.
2. They fix up their drill and set to work.
3. Driller tells his mate he can smell gas, but his mate ignores his warning.
4. Driller chokes and collapses.
5. The others go to help him.
6. The gas fumes increase—the miners choke and struggle and fall.
7. The leader just manages to press the Alarm button.
8. Rescuers come in with gas masks. In turn each of the miners is tied to a rope and dragged out to safety.

Music

'Mars' from Holst's 'Planets' Suite.

Group Leader:

Read this through with your group, decide which idea you like best, and make your own 'Disaster' Play.

JUNGLE 'PLANE CRASH

Medical supplies urgently needed by explorers in jungle who have been attacked and wounded by savages—radio message received at H.Q.—'plane sets out—crashes—crew captured by savages—rescued just in time by explorers.

ABANDON SHIP!

Oil tanker strikes a submerged wreck—starts to sink—crew send out S.O.S. and take to lifeboat—days later they are dying from thirst—see ship—signal and row towards it—it's their own ship still afloat—go aboard—repair it and sail home.

LATE NIGHT EXPRESS

Passengers board train—settle down, sleep—train crashes, throwing passengers about—one little man takes charge—gets people out of carriage though hurt himself—runs to farm for help—he and farmer bring back blankets and hot drinks—suddenly the little man falls and dies.

Make a list of the people.
Cast it from your Group.
Talk over how you are going to act it.

Sound Effects

Jungle Noises and Tree Felling.
Ships and Rain.
Trains (all effects).

CLOCKWORK ARREST!

People

TOYSHOP KEEPER, an old man
ROBBER, a young man
CLOCKWORK SOLDIER
CLOCKWORK GOLLIWOG
CLOCKWORK POLICEMAN
Other clockwork dolls or customers as required.

Place

A toy shop. The three dolls sit side by side. A small safe is near the counter.

Plan of Action

1. Robber comes in. He pretends to be interested in the toys but is really checking for a robbery.
2. The keeper winds up the soldier who marches up and down. [*He can show off the other dolls to this customer—or to other customers.*]
3. Robber goes. Keeper locks up, lights his candle, and goes up to bed.
4. The soldier winds up the golliwog who leaps around him as he marches up and down.
5. As the robber creeps in the dolls stop and watch.
6. While the robber is busy the golliwog carefully moves to the policeman and winds him up. (*See 'Springboard'.*)
7. The policeman knocks out the robber with his truncheon.
8. All the dolls dance joyfully round the fallen robber.
9. They hear the keeper coming and return to their places.
10. The astonished keeper finds the robber, examines his dolls for damage and—puzzled and excited—'phones the police.

Music

Either 'The Funeral Dance of a Marionette', or 'La Boutique
  Fantasque, Part One'.

About this play

This play works very well as a Mime.
With the right music, it is also very effective as a Music Mime.
But you can have *dialogue* in Actions 1 and 2 where the shop-
keeper talks to his customers.

SPRINGBOARD

Group Leader:

Get your Group to look back at Action 6.
You can make this more dramatic to act and more interesting—and
funnier—to watch. Like this:

As soon as the robber comes in the dolls stop dancing.
The robber is a little surprised to see them standing there and
looks at them carefully.
When he starts to work on the safe, the golliwog moves—a
little.
The robber loooks round suspiciously—the golliwog 'freezes'.
Robber works again, and the doll moves again.
Repeat until the golliwog has moved some way.
Robber gets up and inspects the dolls, puzzled.
He paces out the distance from the safe to where the doll *was*,
and to where he is *now*.
Golliwog winds up the policeman—and the robber hears the
winding-noises. He looks round.
The policeman moves towards him—perhaps going in circles,
getting nearer and nearer, and...

This is how you can build up the Actions. Now try it out.

31

PAINTING HOLIDAY
A Comedy

People
TOM SAWYER, a young American boy
AUNT POLLY, his aunt

SID
BEN ROGERS
BILLY
JOHNNY } *Boys*
HARRY
DICK
JIM

JOHNNY *can be played by* SID; JIM *by* SID *or* AUNT POLLY;
HARRY *by* BEN; *and* DICK *by* BILLY. *Or you can join with
another Group: two Leaders cast the parts.*

Place
Aunt Polly's back room. A long fence outside.

Plan of Action
1. Aunt Polly catches Tom taking food from the larder.
2. She sends him out with a pail of whitewash and a brush to paint the fence.
3. Tom is miserable. He paints a little and sits. Aunt Polly shouts—and Tom jumps up.
4. Sid passes with water pails. Tom tries to swop jobs.
5. Aunt Polly creeps up and smacks Tom with a slipper. Sid runs off while Tom works energetically.
6. Soon he sits, dejected. Slowly his face brightens with an idea. He works as if he enjoyed it.
7. Ben Rogers comes along, pretending to be a steam-boat. 'Ting a-ling a-ling! Set her back on the starboard. Ling a-ling-ling! Chow! Ch-chow-chow-chow!'

8. He is astonished to see Tom working. Tom convinces him that it is fun. Ben wants to try.
9. He offers Tom the remainder of his apple. Reluctantly Tom hands him the brush and settles comfortably to eat the apple.
10. Billy comes by, flying a kite. He stares at Ben, then calls Johnny to come and look.
11. Ben insists it's not work—it's a treat. They want to try. Billy offers his kite and Johnny twelve marbles and a bit of blue bottle-glass. Tom accepts.
12. Billy and Johnny each take a turn at painting while Tom watches happily.
13. In turn, Harry gives Tom a dog-collar, Jim a dead rat on a string, Dick a key, and each paints the fence.
14. Tom tells Aunt Polly that he has finished. She thinks he is lying. She inspects the fence and is delighted. She praises Tom for being a good boy and sends him off with an apple.

About this play

This scene is adapted from Mark Twain's 'Tom Sawyer'. Your Group will find that there are many other scenes in this story which you could prepare for acting.

SPRINGBOARD

Group Leader:

Ask your Group to turn out their pockets (and turn out your own) and perhaps their desks.

Use the things you have for bartering with Tom. Most of these things will be small so you'll have to say something about them when you show Tom.

Like this:

BOY: Hey, Tom, let's have a go!

33

TOM: Well—what will you give me?

BOY: I've got a pen-knife with a broken blade.

Or you can exaggerate what you've got, like this:

BOY: Hey, Tom, let's have a go!

TOM: Well—what have you got?

BOY: I've got a terrific silver knife with five blades and a corkscrew.

And you can easily build up this conversation, like this:

Tom doesn't like some things—and rejects them.

Tom doesn't think *one* thing is worth a go—you offer him two things.

You argue with Tom or the other boys about the turns at painting.

While you wait you comment on the work of others.

Talk this over with your Group and try it out.

GOOD SAM

A story of robbery

People

1ST ROBBER

2ND ROBBER

YOUNG MAN ⎫

OLD MAN ⎬ *These parts can be played by one actor*

TRAVELLER

GOOD SAM, a young man

Place

A winding, rock-strewn path. *It is early morning.*

Plan of Action

1. 1st robber sleeps against a rock, his feet towards the embers of a fire.
2. 2nd robber comes in stretching and yawning and rubbing his hands with the cold. He puffs the embers alight— the heat rouses the sleeper. He hops around angrily.
3. They quarrel. They see the traveller coming. They put out the fire and hide.
4. As traveller comes on with his pack 1st robber strolls out and talks to him. They sit on a rock and traveller shows robber his goods.
5. 2nd robber moves from rock to rock to get behind traveller. Suddenly he strikes him down with his dagger.
6. They search the pack and the traveller. They share the spoils gleefully.
7. They see an old man coming. They rush off.
   (*If necessary the robbers can now play other parts.*)
8. The old man sees the traveller who moans for help. He hastens on, afraid of being attacked himself.

35

9. A young man comes on. Seeing the traveller he kneels beside him, takes his dagger, and runs off.

10. Good Sam comes on. He hurries over to the traveller and cleans and binds his wounds. They go off, the traveller supported by Good Sam.

Music

Either 'Dance Macabre', or Beethoven's Pastoral Symphony (storm scene).

About this play

You will probably recognise this story now. It is the Parable of the Good Samaritan.

SPRINGBOARD

Group Leader:

Ask your Group if they can think of their own beginning to this play instead of Actions 1, 2 and 3.

If they can, rehearse it.

What about how the Traveller is attacked?

There are plenty of ways of doing this. Talk them over and try them out.

What about the young man and the old man in Actions 8 and 9? What else could they do?

Remember, this play works very well as a Mime *or as a* Music Mime.

But you can use dialogue, *especially between the robbers; then there will be the Traveller's cries for help and Good Sam talking to him. If you like the play and the words you use, write them down afterwards.*

UNLUCKY FIND

A story of treasure

People

LEADER OF THE HIKERS
TOM
BILL
OTHER HIKERS

Place

In the country. An old well, with a low wall round it, nearby.

Plan of Action

1. The hikers walk on. They are hot and tired. They take off their packs and settle down to eat and rest.
2. Tom wanders off and falls into the well. He calls for help.
3. The others search for him. Bill finds him.
4. The leader takes a rope from his pack and lowers it down the well.
5. Tom calls up to say that he has found a box with money inside.
6. The boys at the top get very excited and insist on the box coming up first.
7. The hikers go off delightedly with the box—leaving Tom calling for help.

Music

Percy Grainger's 'Country Gardens'.
Or a good instrumental record (without lyrics) of your own choice.

SPRINGBOARD

Group Leader:
Ask your Group if they like the ending of this play. If they don't, see

what ideas they have about changing Action 7. Perhaps this will help. Look back at Action 5.

Tom finds a box containing money. Well—what *else* could he find down there?

Decide what he does find.

Decide what he does with it.

Decide what his friends do about the new thing Tom finds.

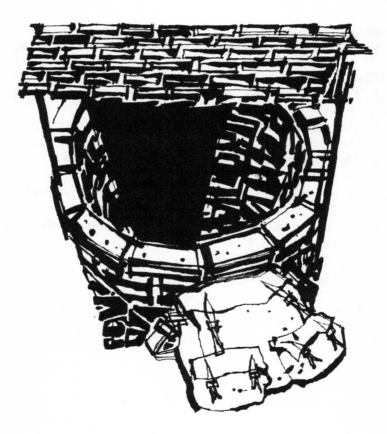

THE IVORY HUNTERS

People

TWO IVORY HUNTERS
TWO GAME WARDENS
NATIVE TRACKERS   *Can be played by one actor*

Place

The African Bush. Camps of the Hunters and the Wardens.

Plan of Action

1. Wardens' camp. They are getting their evening meal. One of them is uneasy and disturbed, perhaps even afraid, about something.
2. A tracker runs in to tell them about the Ivory Hunters up on the hill.
3. The Wardens watch the Hunters through binoculars and decide to track them the next day to stop them killing elephants.
4. Hunters' camp. They are cleaning their guns and stacking up the elephants' tusks they have got. They begin to quarrel about one that they wounded but didn't bring down—the biggest one yet.
5. A tracker tells them about the Game Wardens in the valley.
6. They decide to make an early start the next day and try to shake them off. If they can't they will ambush them.
7. Morning. Guided by their trackers the Wardens follow the Hunters.
8. The Hunters wait in ambush and capture the Wardens. They tie them up and leave them to die. The tracker runs off.
9. The Hunters find the legendary Elephants' Graveyard— the lost valley where the elephants come to die. They go

mad with delight at the sight of so many great ivory tusks.

10. The elephant they had wounded, now dying, charges in. (*See 'Springboard' about acting this scene.*) They try to shoot it down but it tramples them.

11. The frightened tracker returns and frees the Wardens. They go off, leaving the Graveyard in peace.

SPRINGBOARD

Look back at Action 10. A dying elephant charges in. How are you going to manage this?

The audience will not see an elephant so you will have to show them what is happening by your actions, and (if this is an Improvisation) by what you say.

1ST HUNTER: What's that noise?

2ND HUNTER: Where's it coming from?

TRACKER: Massa, Massa, dere's big elephant a-comin'.

1ST HUNTER: Quick, Johnson, over here!

[*They crouch down and raise their rifles.*]

2ND HUNTER: Look out! Here he comes—fire! fire!

1ST HUNTER: He's not stopping! Run for it!

[*They run and fall, raising their hands to protect themselves. Suddenly they lie still.*]

Try this out and then act the play again.

Writing the Play

After you have acted the play several times using your own words, write down the words you said as well as some of the things you did.

Share out the work

—*the Hunters write down their words.*

—*the Wardens write down their words.*

—*the Trackers write down their words.*

NOISES IN THE NIGHT

People

DAD

MUM

BURGLAR

JOE, a boy

DAVE, his friend...can also play Policeman

OTHER FRIENDS or POLICEMEN as required

Place

A house. A field nearby.

Plan of Action

1. Joe and Dave catch a rabbit in the fields.
2. They toss for it and Joe wins. But he's worried about taking it home because his parents do not like pets.
3. Joe smuggles the rabbit up to his bedroom. During supper he asks if he can have a pet but his parents will not let him.
4. Joe goes to bed. He feeds the rabbit with some bread from supper. Then his parents come up to bed.
5. All is quiet. Joe slips out of bed to see the rabbit and discovers that it has got out of the room (perhaps his mother left the door open after saying good-night).
6. Joe creeps downstairs to find it.
7. Mum hears a noise—and wakes Dad. (*See 'Springboard' about acting this scene.*) Mum 'phones the police while Dad goes downstairs.
8. Joe hides while his Dad searches the house. The police arrive—and Joe is found. He explains about the rabbit—everyone is angry.
9. The rabbit runs out of the house. Joe chases after it, Mum and Dad run out after Joe, and the police follow.

10. Police catch a real burglar coming out of a window of the house. Joe recaptures the rabbit.
11. Everyone (except the burglar!) is pleased. The police because they have caught a burglar, Mum and Dad because they've got their things back, and Joe because they let him keep the rabbit as a reward.

SPRINGBOARD

Look back at Action 7. 'Mum hears a noise and wakes Dad.' Then she 'phones the police while Dad goes off to find out what the noises are. *This Action can be built up to make a good comic scene. Read the following, discuss it, and act Action 7 again.*

What would Mum say?

George...George...wake up, George!

What would Dad say?

Aarhumm! Go to sleep, Mabel....

What would Mum do?

Shake him.

George, I can hear someone moving about—downstairs.

What would Dad do?

Grunt. Snore. Turn over.

How does she get him up?

She tips him out of bed. Or more shaking.

How does Dad feel now?

Well, not very pleased. Cross. Perhaps angry.

What on earth's the matter with you, Mabel—throwing me out of bed in the middle of the night.

How does Mum feel now?

A bit worried in case he's hurt himself in falling.
A bit upset herself because he's cross.
And a bit frightened about the noises she can hear.

42

Does Dad want to go downstairs?

If you play him as a big, tough man he won't mind.

Never you mind, Mabel, I'll fix him. Blinking burglars
creeping about my house knocking off stuff!

If you play him as a weak, timid little fellow he might be a little reluctant.

No, no, Mabel, you must be dreaming. There's no one
there. 'Course I'm not scared. I'm shivering because
it's cold standing around here listening.

So you can see that a lot depends on how you play these parts.

Talk over this scene.

Decide how you are going to play your parts.

Now try the play again.

KNOCK OUT!

A story about a boxing match

People

CAULIFLOWER BILL, a very confident boxing champion
JOE, a not very confident challenger
SECONDS, retired boxers who assist Bill and Joe
REFEREE ⎫
ANNOUNCER ⎭ *can be played by one actor*

Place

A boxing ring. Stools in opposite corners.

Plan of Action

1. The great contest is announced giving details of names, weigh-in, number of rounds, names of time-keeper and referee.
2. The Champ walks to the ring and climbs in to loud cheers. He feels certain he will win.
3. Joe walks to the ring and climbs in reluctantly. He feels he has already lost.
4. Seconds get the contestants ready.
5. Referee calls the contestants to the centre of the ring. He inspects their gloves and asks for a clean fight. Joe and Bill shake hands and return to their corners.
6. Bell sounds. In round one Joe keeps well out of Bill's way. Joe's nervousness helps to increase Bill's confidence. Bell.
7. Seconds work on Joe and Bill.
8. Bell sounds. In round two Bill works hard on Joe's body. A huge swing from him puts Joe down for eight when he is saved by the bell.
9. Seconds work in the corners. Bill is now over-confident — he expects to win by a knock-out.

10. Bell sounds. Third round. Bill is careless—waves to crowd, turns his back on Joe, even puts down his guard.
11. Joe takes his chance. He catches Bill with a terrific blow which knocks him out.
12. Loud cheers for the new Champ. The ex-Champ walks slowly away, all his confidence gone. (*Does Joe care how the ex-Champ feels? What could he do to show sympathy?*)

SPRINGBOARD

Group Leader:

Make sure that your Group understands this before you act the fight.
You must not, of course, strike actual blows. You are acting.
The fighters should rehearse what they are going to do.
They must carefully time the exchange of blows and make sure that they miss.
Each must know what the other is going to do.
Fighting in 'slow-motion' will help.

Now read this and talk it over.

What's the really dramatic thing about this fight?
   How the confident Champion expects *to win—but loses.*
   How the rather fearful Challenger expects *to lose—but wins.*

How does this affect the play?

   1. Bill must *act* his confidence—and his disappointment in defeat.
   2. Joe must *act* his nervousness—and his surprise? delight? pride? in victory.

If the fighters show their feelings (1 and 2) it will make the play a success.

HAPPY CHRISTMAS!

A Play in Two Contrasting Scenes

Each scene can be acted by a Group of five or more.

Group Leader:

Read this with your group before you act this play, or before you act it again:

'Oh! But he was a tight-fisted hand at the grindstone, Scrooge! a squeezing, wrenching, grasping, scraping, clutching, covetous, old sinner! Hard and sharp as flint, from which no steel had ever struck out generous fire; secret, and self-contained, and solitary as an oyster.'

That was Charles Dickens's own description of Scrooge.

And there's more to come! Read the opening chapter of 'A Christmas Carol' to get a full picture of Scrooge. It will help you to see him as something more than an old miser—and to put this into your acting.

It will also give you all the dialogue *for these scenes. Some dialogue is given here, especially in Scene Two.*

46

HAPPY CHRISTMAS!

In Two Scenes

Scene One

People

SCROOGE, an old miser who hates Christmas

SCROOGE'S NEPHEW, a cheerful young man

BOB CRATCHIT, Scrooge's clerk: poor, thin, hungry

ANNOUNCER

1ST GENTLEMAN $\Big\}$ *Can be played by one actor*

2ND GENTLEMAN

CAROL SINGER $\Big\}$ *Can be played by one actor*

Place and Time

Christmas Eve. A cold, foggy day. Scrooge's counting house. Two desks, two high stools. A tiny fire, two candles alight. *The announcer can give changes of place and date.*

Plan of Action

1. Scrooge works at his desk. Bob puts on his scarf and warms his hands at his candle.
2. Scrooge's nephew bursts in cheerfully.
     'A merry Christmas, Uncle!'
3. Scrooge snarls and turns away from him.
     'Bah! Humbug! Every idiot who goes about with "Merry Christmas" on his lips should be boiled with his own pudding, and buried with a stake of holly through his heart!'
4. Nephew laughs and invites him to dinner. Scrooge refuses, wishing him goodbye.
5. Still cheerful, Scrooge's nephew exchanges greetings with Bob, and leaves.
6. Two gentlemen come in. They ask for a donation for the poor at Christmas.

7. Scrooge is indignant. There are prisons and workhouses for the poor. He cannot afford to make idle people merry.
8. They go out, surprised and disappointed.
9. Carol singer begins a carol at the door. Scrooge seizes a ruler and chases him off.
10. Nervously Bob begs Scrooge for Christmas Day off. Scrooge reluctantly agrees—but he must come in all the earlier on Boxing Day.
11. Bob promises. Scrooge goes out with a growl. Bob quickly locks up and rushes off.

This scene and the next can be linked by an announcement.

ANNOUNCER:

Now we see how Scrooge has changed after the visits of the Christmas Ghosts when he learns the real meaning of Christmas.

You can use all *or* some *of the dialogue in this scene, or make up your own.*

Scene Two

People

SCROOGE
BOB CRATCHIT
SCROOGE'S NEPHEW
BOY
1ST GENTLEMAN } *Can be played by one actor*
2ND GENTLEMAN
ANNOUNCER } *Can be played by one actor*

Place and Time

Scrooge's bedroom. Christmas morning.

48

Plan of Action

1. Scrooge leaps joyfully out of bed. He dresses in a rush, mixing up his clothes, turning them inside out, putting them on the wrong way round, tearing them, losing them, and laughing all the while.

SCROOGE: I don't know what to do! I am as light as a feather, I am as happy as an angel, I am as merry as a schoolboy. I am as giddy as a drunken man....A Merry Christmas to everybody! A Happy New Year to all the world. Hallo there! Whoop! Hallo!

2. Church bells ring. Scrooge listens, throws up the window and looks around happily.

SCROOGE: Ah! no fog, no mist—golden sunlight—merry bells—glorious, glorious!

3. He calls to a passing boy.

SCROOGE: What's to-day?

BOY: Eh?

SCROOGE: What's to-day, my fine fellow?

BOY: To-day? Why, to-day's Christmas Day.

SCROOGE: It's Christmas Day! I haven't missed it. Do you know the Poulterer's at the corner of the street?

BOY: I should think I did.

SCROOGE: Do you know whether they have sold the prize turkey that was hanging up there?

BOY: What—the one as big as me?

SCROOGE: Yes, my lad!

BOY: It's hanging there now.

SCROOGE: Is it? Go and buy it.

BOY: Go on!

SCROOGE: No, no—I mean it. Here's the money. Go and buy it—and I'll give you half-a-crown!

4. He throws money to the boy and tells him to take the turkey to Bob Cratchit's. The boy runs off.

5. Boxing Day morning. Scrooge whistles cheerfully as he walks to his office. He gives a little joyful dance every now and then, laughing aloud.

6. He meets the two gentlemen, shakes their hands warmly —much to their surprise—and gives them money as his Christmas Gift.

7. Scrooge bustles into his office, checking his watch against the office clock. He waits, his back turned to the door.

8. Bob rushes in, throws off his scarf, and begins work at once.

9. Scrooge pretends to be angry with him for being late. Bob apologises humbly.

10. Suddenly Scrooge's manner changes. He leaps up, digs Bob in the ribs—and promises to raise his salary!

11. Bob retreats, frightened—Scrooge has gone mad!

12. Laughing, Scrooge slaps him on the back and asks him to make up a huge fire. Astonished but delighted, Bob does so.

13. Scrooge's nephew comes in. Scrooge shakes his hand and begs to be allowed to come to dinner.

14. His nephew is overjoyed. He produces a small bottle of wine. Bob finds some glasses. They drink to Christmas and the new Scrooge.

Scene Changes

The actions in Scene Two occur in three places:
Scrooge's bedroom.
The Street.
Scrooge's Office.

Design your own set to show these three places at the same time.

SPRINGBOARD

Group Leader:

When you have acted these two scenes you will notice that they show two pictures of Scrooge.

Like an advertisement for a cold cure, they show you 'Before' and 'After'.

In Scene One he is mean and hates Christmas.

In Scene Two he is generous and loves Christmas.

So the two scenes show how Scrooge's character changes.

His character changes because Scrooge has learnt from the Ghosts of Christmas Past, Christmas Present and Christmas Future, what Christmas really means.

A 'Contrast' Play in Two Scenes for your Group

Here are some ideas to work on.

A quiet scene (*campers going to sleep*); then—A noisy, active scene (*a storm wrecks the tent*).

A cruel, selfish boy; then—A kind, helpful boy.

You can also have a Third Scene, between these two, to show why *the boy changes.*

One of the Ghost scenes from 'A Christmas Carol' then—Bob Cratchit's Christmas Party.

The contrast here is between a gloomy, frightening scene and a warm, merry one.

Decide which idea you like best (or think of your own).

Talk over what is going to happen.

Write down an outline of what happens.

Cast the play, and try it out.

THE TRAVELLING COMPANION

In Five Scenes

Each scene can be played by a Group of five or more.
If each scene is played by different Groups, the whole form
can take part.

Full Cast

JOHN	KING
TRAVELLING COMPANION	PRINCESS
1ST GRAVEDIGGER	MAGICIAN
2ND GRAVEDIGGER	MAGICIAN'S SERVANTS
OLD WOMAN	GUARDS
SHOWMAN	PUPPETS
SERVANTS	

Scenes

1. A Churchyard.
2. In the country, near the King's Palace.
3. The Palace courtyard. *Evening.*
4. The same. *Midnight.*
5. Courtyard of the Palace.

Scene One

People

JOHN
TWO GRAVE DIGGERS
TRAVELLING COMPANION
OLD WOMAN

Place

A Churchyard.

Plan of Action

1. The two men are digging up a grave.

2. John comes in carrying a knapsack on his back. He sits down wearily on a wall.

3. John asks them what they are doing. They explain roughly that the dead man cheated them out of their money by dying before paying them. Their revenge is to leave him to lie outside the church door so that all will know he was a cheat.

4. John gives them fifty pieces of silver—all he has—to leave the dead man in peace.

5. They look at him in astonishment. They seize the money and count it greedily.

6. They go off laughing at John's foolish good nature.

7. John sets the grave in order and then rests his head in his hands.

8. The Travelling Companion greets John cheerfully. He offers to keep John company and they settle down to eat together.

9. An old woman limps on. She carries a great bundle of sticks on her back. As she passes she stumbles.

10. John jumps up and catches her. She sits down painfully.

11. The Companion rubs her leg with an ointment from his knapsack. In return he asks for three fern stems from her bundle which she gives him.

12. She gets up and goes off, walking quite springily.

Scene Two

People

JOHN
TRAVELLING COMPANION
SHOWMAN
PUPPETS...*according to numbers*

Place

In the country, near the King's Palace.

Plan of Action

1. John and the Travelling Companion pass a Showman. He stands, dejected, beside his puppets lying scattered on the ground near a broken cart.

2. John offers to help mend the puppets. The Showman is grateful. The Companion offers to make the puppets move and talk like living creatures in exchange for the Showman's old sword.

3. The Showman picks up a puppet who hangs limply. The Companion rubs in the ointment.

4. On the Companion's command the puppet begins to dance jerkily. The Showman is delighted.

5. Faint groans come from the other puppets—they want to be repaired and to dance by themselves.

6. Each is picked up, straightened out and rubbed. They dance happily.

7. The Showman warns them about the King's wicked but very beautiful daughter. She asks her suitor's three questions. If he answers correctly he may marry her and share the kingdom. If he fails, his head is cut off. Already many have failed.

8. John and his Companion set off for the Palace.

Scene Three

People

JOHN
TRAVELLING COMPANION
KING
PRINCESS
GUARDS

Place

The Palace courtyard. *Evening*.

Plan of Action

1. John and the Travelling Companion knock at the Palace door.
2. The Princess passes. John is amazed at her beauty.
3. The old King, untidy and sad, comes out. He carries his sceptre and orb.
4. They shake hands and John offers to become his daughter's suitor.
5. King drops his sceptre and orb and bursts into tears which he wipes away on his dressing gown.
6. He begs John not to risk his life.
7. The Princess returns, John bows low, she offers him her hand and he kisses it.
8. He can make his trial the next morning. She walks on, John gazing after.
9. The Companion and John drink to success. John is in high spirits, unaware of his danger. The Companion offers to help him.
10. John feels sleepy. The Companion sends him off to rest. The Companion waits in the courtyard.

Scene Four

People

TRAVELLING COMPANION

PRINCESS

MAGICIAN

MAGICIAN'S SERVANTS: Goblins
Snakes
Bats
Animals
Monsters

According to numbers

Place

The Palace Courtyard. *Midnight.*

Plan of Action

1. The Companion stands hidden in an archway watching. A clock strikes twelve.
2. The Princess comes in wrapped in a long cloak. She waits and looks about.
3. The Companion lashes her across the shoulders with the fern-rods. She cowers under his blows, thinking it hailstones. She does not see him.
4. The Magician suddenly appears. The Princess curtsies.
5. The Magician's servants dance wildly round them.
6. The Magician tells her to think of her shoes, her gloves and the Magician's head. John must guess her thoughts as she thinks of each one. She must bring him John's eyes when he is executed.
7. The Princess goes.
8. The Companion springs upon the Magician and kills him with his sword.
9. All the creatures vanish.
10. The Companion cuts off the Magician's head and wraps it in a cloth.

56

Scene Five

People

JOHN
TRAVELLING COMPANION
KING
PRINCESS
SERVANTS
GUARDS } (*Not essential. Cast if numbers available.*)

Place

Courtyard of the Palace. *The following morning.*

Plan of Action

1. John comes in whistling cheerfully and greets the Companion. He is very confident.
2. Companion tells him about the Princess's glove and shoe. He gives him the tied cloth, to answer the third question.
3. The King, Princess, servants and guards come in.
4. John answers the first two questions. At each the people applaud. The King is delighted, the Princess looks faint.
5. To answer the third question he opens the cloth. The court gasps in horror. The Princess faints.
6. The King begs John not to marry the Princess as she is still evil and cruel.
7. The Companion instructs John to beat the Princess with the fern rods to destroy the power of the Magician over her.
8. Reluctantly he does so. She writhes, cries out and then lies still. She rises smiling and goes to John. Everyone is delighted.
9. The Companion says goodbye to John; he must go now that his debt to him is paid. John looks at him, astonished and puzzled.

57

10. The Companion reminds John of the money he gave to the grave diggers so that the dead man could rest in peace. He is that man. He disappears in the crowd.
11. They scatter to find him, but he has vanished. They all stand looking and calling after him.

About this Play
This play is based on a Hans Andersen story. There is a complete script of this play, written by a Second Year form on page 75.

SPRINGBOARD
Group Leader:
You will find that it is fairly easy to make up words for this play (if you do it as an Improvisation).

Ask your Group if they think some music would help. Look through the scenes and find which scenes would be helped by music. Then look under the 'Music' heading for some suggestions.
Next—
ask the Group to choose the scene they like most.
Work on the scene they choose to give a really 'finished' performance.
Like this:
Take each Action in turn—talk about it—get suggestions from your members—rehearse this one Action until you're satisfied with it. Then go on to the next Action.
At the end you should have a scene that's worth showing to the rest of the class.

Music
Music will help the playing and the effect of scenes two and four. *If you think you would like music in other scenes you can decide what you would like.*
In Scene Two the dance of the puppets can be suggested by 'The Funeral Dance of a Marionette'.

In Scene Four the opening passage of 'Dance Macabre' will suggest the striking of the clock at midnight, while the power of the magician and the evil of the Princess are excitingly conveyed by 'A Night on the Bare Mountain'.

THE SWORD AND THE DRAGON
In Five Scenes

*The first four scenes can be played by a Group of five or more.
For the last scene you will have to borrow members from another
Group or double-up with one.*

Full Cast

BLACKSMITH
BLACKSMITH'S WIFE
PAUL ⎫
HUGH ⎬ Their three sons
RALPH ⎭
KING'S HERALD
AN OLD CRONE
DRAGON
STONE
PRINCESS
KING
QUEEN
VILLAGERS

Scenes

1. The market square and Blacksmith's house.
2. Blacksmith's forge and woods.
3. The same.
4. The same.
5. The market square.

Group Leader:

*There is no need to change the set for each scene of this play. Appoint
one member of your Group to design on paper, or to arrange with the
things you have, a simple set which can be used, with very few changes,
for all the scenes.*

60

Scene One

People

BLACKSMITH

BLACKSMITH'S WIFE: proud of Paul and Hugh, rather ashamed of Ralph

PAUL, vain, conceited, smartly-dressed, hates work

HUGH, big and strong, does exercises, very proud of his strength

RALPH, a dreamer, always lost in thought, people think him a fool

KING'S HERALD (*Wife could also play this part.*)

VILLAGERS (*if actors available*)

Place

The market square. We can see the Blacksmith's forge, inside his house next door and the market square.

Plan of Action

1. Blacksmith busy at his forge making ploughshares and fine sharp knives.
2. His little wife swiftly whisks her twig broom and dusts everything, darting about like a bird.
3. Outside Paul parades in his fine clothes. His mother calls to him to help her. He turns away—he would spoil his clothes or damage his finger-nails.
4. Nearby Hugh is doing exercises with a log. His mother calls to him. He turns a cartwheel and stays in a hand-stand position. (*He could use the broom for exercises.*)
5. Ralph rests by a tree in the square. He wanders round the square humming to himself. His mother calls. He drifts round the house, starts to sweep, picks up a book and begins to read. His mother angrily snatches back the broom.

6. Now in the square the villagers are shopping, buying, selling, gossiping, enjoying the sun.
   (*Leave this out if short of actors. But you could borrow some from another Group.*)

7. A trumpet sounds. The square falls silent. Everyone gathers round the Herald. The Princess is held prisoner by the terrible Dragon. Her rescuer may marry her and receive half the Kingdom.

8. The villagers are excited by this news. They go about their business discussing how the Dragon may be slain. But no one seems very anxious to go.

Scene Two

People

BLACKSMITH
BLACKSMITH'S WIFE
PAUL, the proud, well-dressed son
AN OLD CRONE
DRAGON (*one or more players*)
STONE with a sword in it (*Wife could play this part. Cover the actor with a blanket. You need not have an actor for this part at all — but you can get a good comic effect if you do.*)

Place

Blacksmith's forge and woods.

Plan of Action

1. Blacksmith makes a bar of metal red-hot. He beats it, wipes the sweat from his brow and beats again. He plunges the bar into a tub of water. He fixes on the hand-guard and sharpens the blade on a wheel.

62

2. He practises sword-play: lunge, thrust, parry, retreat, advance, cut, slash. He jumps back—and falls awkwardly.

3. He groans with pain, clutching his ankle.

4. His wife dashes in and fusses over him. How will they earn their living now? Someone must slay the Dragon and gain half the kingdom—especially as the Blacksmith has made a sword for this purpose.

5. Though he protests greatly, Paul is made to go. He sets off with some sandwiches, holding the sword daintily before him.

6. He glides through the woods, carefully avoiding the rough twigs that snatch at his fine clothes.

7. He reaches a cave. Nearby is a stone with a magnificent sword embedded in it. He carefully spreads a silk handkerchief on a rock and sits on it to eat his food.

8. The old crone appears and begs for a crust. Paul spurns her, disgusted by her rags. She offers to tell him the secret of the sword in exchange for bread but he waves her away.

9. The Dragon slithers from the cave. Paul is too frightened to run. The Dragon is old and cunning, victor of many battles. He praises Paul's fine clothes:
   'How splendid you look in your fine clothes. Pray, walk about a little that my old eyes may see you more clearly.'

10. Paul parades proudly, forgetting his task and his danger. He draws closer to the Dragon who springs forward and bites his leg.

11. Paul wrenches himself away and goes limping home as fast as he can to be comforted by his mother.

Scene Three

People

BLACKSMITH

BLACKSMITH'S WIFE

HUGH, the strong son

OLD CRONE

DRAGON

STONE with a sword in it (*can be played by Blacksmith or wife*)

PAUL (*can be played by Old Crone*)

Place

Blacksmith's house, indoors, and woods with cave and stone.

Plan of Action

1. The wife bandages Paul's leg and props it up on a chair. She is in despair—what can they do now?
2. The second son, Hugh, must go. Blacksmith—now just able to stand—tries to show Hugh how to use the sword.
3. But Hugh brushes the advice aside: he hasn't built up his muscles for nothing. Full of confidence—but taking the sword 'just in case'—he sets off.
4. At the cave he sits to eat his sandwiches. The old crone begs for a crust.
5. Hugh retorts that he needs all the food he can get for himself, to keep up his strength, to build up his muscles.
6. She offers to tell him the secret of the sword in the stone in return for food. Hugh waves her away, confident that he is strong enough to do it himself.
7. He heaves, wrenches, strains, until he falls exhausted. (*Here, if you have an actor covered by a blanket as the stone, you can add to the comedy of this scene. As Hugh pulls on the sword the stone can slide along—with the sword remaining in place.*) He eats some more, tries again, but fails to move the sword.

8. The Dragon slips silently from his cave.
   'Why, what a splendid-looking visitor I have here!
   Pray, show me your strength, and skill that my old eyes
   may see how fine you are.'
9. Hugh is delighted. He leaps and springs, flexes his
   muscles and cartwheels round, coming closer and closer
   to the Dragon.
10. The Dragon bites him; Hugh rushes home to be comforted
    by his mother.

Scene Four

People

BLACKSMITH
BLACKSMITH'S WIFE
RALPH, the dreamer
OLD CRONE
DRAGON
STONE with a sword in it (*can be played by Blacksmith*)
PRINCESS (*can be played by Wife*)
PAUL (*can be played by Old Crone*)
HUGH (*can be played by Dragon*)

Place

Blacksmith's house, indoors, and woods with cave and stone.

Plan of Action

1. The wife bandages Hugh's leg and props it up beside
   Paul's injured leg. What can they do now? Still limping, the Blacksmith bravely offers to try—but his wife
   will not let him go.
2. Ralph offers to go. How they laugh! But they agree
   that if he wants to go he may. Taking the sword in one
   hand and a book in the other, Ralph sets off.
3. As he goes his mother gathers sticks and sadly ties two
   together—to make a cross! She doesn't expect to see him
   alive again. (*You can add to the comedy here. Ralph is such a*

65

dreamer that he doesn't know that his brothers have been off fighting a dragon; he doesn't even know where the woods are! He wanders round—and returns home several times.)

4. When he reaches the cave Ralph drops sleepily onto the ground. Presently he rouses himself to eat his sandwiches.

5. Now the old crone appears; Ralph offers her a sandwich.

6. She throws off her ragged cloak to reveal—Merlin, the Magician. He touches the sword in the stone. Ralph draws it free easily.

7. The Dragon, sensing danger, charges out to attack Ralph. Retreating all the time, he lashes out with the sword, but the Dragon is too quick and too clever for him.

8. Ralph tumbles over the stone. The Dragon springs at him.

9. Merlin momentarily diverts the Dragon's attention by making a noise (*or a sudden movement*). Ralph swings the sword—and the Dragon is dead.

10. Now the Princess runs from the cave (*or she could watch the fight. Her reactions to the contest would add to the dramatic effect of this scene.*) Hand-in-hand the Princess and the Dreamer run back to the village.

Scene Five

People

To play this scene a group will have to join with or borrow members from another group.

BLACKSMITH	KING
BLACKSMITH'S WIFE	QUEEN
PAUL	HERALD
HUGH	OLD CRONE
RALPH	VILLAGERS
PRINCESS	

Place

The village square.

Plan of Action

1. As Ralph and the Princess come into the square people stop and stare in astonishment. They call to their friends.
2. Out limps the Blacksmith, followed by his wife and Paul and Hugh. At first they cannot believe their eyes.
3. The Blacksmith bows to the Princess and shakes Ralph's hand warmly. The villagers cheer madly and gather round the pair, congratulating them.
4. The Herald appears and sounds his trumpet. Everyone falls silent, waiting expectantly.
5. The King and Queen come in. The villagers bow and curtsy as they pass. They are overjoyed to see their daughter. They praise Ralph's courage—and the marriage date is set.
6. The villagers cheer and dance round the happy pair as night falls; only the sword, held aloft by Ralph, glows mysteriously in the moonlight.

SPRINGBOARD

Group Leader:

Did your Group find this an easy story to follow and to act? If they did they should not find it difficult to make up one like it.
Here are some things to help you.

This is a 'pattern' play—certain things happen again and again, but in slightly different ways. Each of the sons is asked to sweep up, each of the sons goes off to fight the dragon....

Any more? Ask your Group. It will help your own play later.
Another thing—each of the sons is different. Paul is proud

of his smart clothes. *Look at Action 6 in Scene Two to see how he goes through the woods.*

What are the other sons like? Ask your Group.

Finally, notice which son kills the dragon. It is not Hugh, the strong son, but the *most unlikely.*

Now for your 'pattern' play

Decide on three people (*boys, girls, adults*).

Decide how they are different (*looks, brains, skills*).

Decide what they are to try to do (*find something, rescue, capture or kill something*).

Decide how the first two people fail, and how the third succeeds.

Music

'Live' music would be best. A group of recorders and a drum would be effective; so, too, would a piano as an accompaniment to the action and assisting, perhaps, a narrator. Extracts from Humperdinck's 'Hansel and Gretel' would be suitable for the village and home scenes.

THE GREAT LEADER

A story of Moses. In Four Scenes

Full Cast

MOSES

AARON, his brother

EGYPTIAN TASKMASTER

ELI

JOSEPH

AMOS   } *Jewish slaves*

MICHAEL

PHARAOH

SERVANT

HASIM, a spy

PRINCESS, foster mother of Moses

CAPTAIN OF PHARAOH'S GUARDS

1ST SOLDIER

2ND SOLDIER

3RD SOLDIER

Other Soldiers and Guards

Scenes 1, 3 and 4 can be acted by a Group of five or more. Scene 2 needs only three actors.

Scene One

People

TASKMASTER

ELI

JOSEPH

MOSES

HASIM

Place

A pyramid building site.

69

Plan of Action

1. The Taskmaster watches the Hebrew slaves straining to move slabs of stones. He drives them on with a whip.
2. Eli falls and begs for water. The Taskmaster threatens him.
3. Joseph helps Eli up. The Taskmaster drives Joseph away.
4. Eli sways and falls, ripping the Taskmaster's tunic as he does so.
5. The Taskmaster is furious. He flogs Eli mercilessly.
6. Moses rushes forward angrily to stop the beating.
7. A spy, Hasim, is following Moses. He watches from behind a rock.
8. Moses snatches the whip and strikes the Taskmaster.
9. The Taskmaster rushes at Moses with drawn sword. Moses kicks up the sand, blinding him, then kills him with his dagger. (*Or he might use the whip to snatch the sword away from the Taskmaster.*)
10. Moses's anger cools—he realises what he has done. He quickly buries the body in the sand and hurries off.
11. Hasim watches him leave, then begins to uncover the body ...

Scene Two

People

AMOS
MICHAEL
MOSES

Place

Near the Jewish Camp.

Plan of Action

1. Amos accuses Michael of stealing the mud bricks he has made. Michael denies this.

70

2. Amos hits Michael. They fight and roll on the ground.

3. Moses separates them and orders them to stop quarrelling.

4. They turn on him, accusing him of murder. Eli has told them how he, Moses, killed the Taskmaster.

5. Moses is afraid of the Pharaoh's vengeance and must escape.

6. They promise to help him because he saved Eli from the taskmaster. Moses hurries off.

Scene Three

People
PHARAOH

PRINCESS

HASIM

SERVANT

GUARDS

Place
The Pharaoh's Palace.

Plan of Action

1. Servant tells Pharaoh that Hasim has vital information.

2. Guards escort Hasim forward. Hasim reports the death of the Taskmaster.

3. Pharaoh is very angry and demands the name of the killer.

4. Pharaoh cannot believe that it is Moses. He orders his guards to bring the body and Eli as evidence.

5. The Princess pleads with Pharaoh for Moses's life.

6. Guards hustle her away while Pharaoh orders a search for Moses.

71

Scene Four

People

MOSES   1ST SOLDIER
AARON   2ND SOLDIER *(can also play Aaron)*
CAPTAIN   3RD SOLDIER

Place

Somewhere in the desert.

Plan of Action

1. Moses staggers in exhausted. He crawls to a group of rocks and hides.
2. In the distance the soldiers search for him.
3. The Captain orders two soldiers to search the rocks where Moses is hidden. The Captain and 3rd soldier go off.
4. The soldiers rest on the rocks instead of searching. 1st soldier drinks from water bottle.
5. Moses reaches up, drinks from the bottle and replaces it.
6. The second soldier finds the water bottle nearly empty. He is very angry and accuses the 1st soldier of greediness.
7. They quarrel and fight with swords.
8. Moses moves away from them.
9. The Captain breaks up the fight. He is angry because they are not searching. The 3rd soldier spots Moses creeping away.
10. The soldiers surround the rocks. Moses jumps onto a high rock, his dagger in his hand. *(Rehearse 11, 12, 13, carefully.)*
11. 3rd soldier leaps at Moses. Before he strikes, Moses stabs him and snatches up his sword.
12. 2nd soldier climbs up behind Moses but misses him. He falls back wounded. *(He could now stagger off-stage to play Aaron, if necessary.)*

13. The Captain strikes Moses in the arm, causing him to drop his sword.

14. Moses waits for the final blow.

15. Aaron charges in, knocks over the Captain and kills him.

16. Moses turns to fight the 1st soldier, who runs off.

17. Aaron binds up his brother's wound with strips of his tunic. He has searched everywhere to warn him.

18. Moses decides to leave Egypt until it is safe to return. He will wait and pray for guidance. He believes that one day he will be able to help the Jews—perhaps set them free.

19. They shake hands. Aaron waves farewell as Moses goes off into the desert.

About this Play

This story is based on a brief incident in the Bible: Exodus 2: verses 11 to 15. If you read these verses you will see how this play has been built up, given more people, and split up into scenes.

The version given here was worked out by a First Year class who also wrote the complete script of the play which begins on page 83.

SPRINGBOARD

Group Leader:

Ask your Group which scene they think is the most exciting to act. Scene Four is exciting because of the fight.

BUT—you will enjoy acting it more, and it will be better to watch, if you talk over these rules and carry them out in this fight and in any other fight.

1. Keep each fight short.
2. Keep each fight as simple as possible.
3. Make sure you know what your opponent is going to do— and when it's going to happen.
4. When you are 'killed', fall down—and stay still.
5. When you are 'wounded', clutch yourself where you are hit; don't fall down, but stagger off the set.
6. Practise 'stage-falls'—that is, falling as if dead when hit.
7. Try out what you are going to do several times in your rehearsals.
8. Go through your fight slowly at first, then gradually increase speed.

THE TRAVELLING COMPANION

A Scripted Play in Five Scenes

Full Cast

THE TRAVELLING COMPANION
JOHN
ALF
JOE
PUPPET MASTER
KING
PRINCESS
MAGICIAN
OLD LADY
MONSTERS AND ANIMALS ⎫
PUPPETS   ⎬ *All according to numbers available*
PALACE GUARDS   ⎭

Scenes

A Graveyard.
In the country.
The Palace.
The Palace Courtyard.
The Palace.
Each scene in this play can be acted by a Group of five or more.

Scene One

Place

A Graveyard.

> [*Two men are digging up a grave.*]

ALF: This is hard work, Joe.

JOE: Yes, I'll be glad when it's finished.

ALF: Still, it serves him right for not paying his debts.

> [*John comes in.*]

JOHN: Good day! What are you doing there?

JOE: We are digging him up.

JOHN: Why?

ALF: Because he owed us money.

JOHN: How much?

JOE: Fifty crowns.

JOHN: Where are you going to put him?

ALF: Outside the church gates.

JOHN: Why do that?

JOE: To show him up.

JOHN: If I give you all my money will you leave him alone?

ALF: How much have you got?

JOHN: Just a minute [*counts*]. I've got forty crowns.

[*Joe and Alf whisper together.*]

JOE: That will be all right.

ALF: [*Taking the money.*] You can cover him up again. Good-bye. [*They go out laughing. John sits down and begins to eat. The Companion comes in and stops.*]

COMP.: Good morning, my friend. I have not had anything to eat, I'm hungry.

JOHN: Sit down and join me. There's enough for two.

COMP.: Thank you, that's kind of you. [*They eat.*] What brings you here?

JOHN: Just now I saw two men digging up a grave.

COMP.: Why?

JOHN: Because they said he owed them some money. So they were going to put him outside the churchyard.

COMP.: What did you do?

JOHN: I gave them all my money to let him rest in peace.

COMP.: That was kind of you. If you don't mind I'll go with you and be your companion.

[*The old lady carrying a large bundle of sticks comes in and falls over.*]

OLD LADY: My leg! my leg! I've hurt my leg! [*John and the Companion go to help her.*]

COMP.: I will help you. I have some ointment here. It will make your leg better. Now, if you give me three of those ferns I will rub on some ointment.

O.L.: What use are those fern sticks to you?

COMP.: You don't know—they may come in handy.

O.L.: All right, you can have them. [*He puts the ointment on her leg and the old lady gets up and walks.*]

O.L.: I feel much better now. Thank you. Good-bye. [*She goes.*]

JOHN: Let's go on our way. [*They go off.*]

Scene Two

Place

In the country. *Broken puppets are scattered about.*

PUPPET MASTER: Dear, oh dear! all my puppets are broken! What shall I do? [*He inspects the broken arms and legs.*]
[*John and the Companion come in.*]

JOHN: What has happened, my friend?

P.M.: My cart hit a stone and all my puppets fell out.

COMP.: I have some ointment in my bag. It will mend all your puppets. It will not only make them better, it will make them like real people. They won't need strings at all!

P.M.: Thank you, kind sir! What can I do to repay you?

COMP.: See that rusty sword by your side?—give me that.

P.M.: This old rusty sword's no good to you. But you can have it if you wish. [*He gives sword to him. The Companion rubs ointment onto puppets. They start to move by themselves.*] What do I do to make them stop?

COMP.: If you say STOP! they will stop. If you say DANCE! they will dance. They will do anything you say. [*The Puppet Master gives orders which the puppets obey.*]

P.M.: Thank you for all you've done. Where are you going my friends?

JOHN: We are going to the Palace.

P.M.: That is a coincidence. I happen to be going there.

COMP.: Let us come along with you. We'll help to look after the puppets.

P.M.: Thank you, my friends, but I must tell you about the Princess first. She is very beautiful but she is also very wicked. She serves an evil magician who gives her three difficult questions to ask the young men who want to marry her. If they don't give the three right answers they have their heads chopped off!

COMP.: Thank you for warning us. Let us go now.

[*They all go off.*]

Scene Three

Place

The Palace.

KING: Oh dear! Oh dear! If you want anything done in this house you have to do it yourself. I ask for bacon and egg and what do I get? Mushrooms!

PRINCESS: Oh, father, you've had your breakfast. You must be going out of your mind.

[*Knock at the door.*]

KING: Thunder! It's thunder. I can't go for a ride now.

PRIN.: Father, it's someone at the door.

GUARD: Someone to see you, sir.

KING: Ask them if they have an appointment. [*The Guard goes out and then returns.*] Well? What did they say?

GUARD: They haven't got an appointment, sir.

KING: Oh, well, let them in. [*Guard does so.*] Who are you? What do you want?

COMP.: This is John and I am his companion. He wants to marry the princess.

KING: I must warn you. I suppose you know that if you fail to answer the three questions she asks you she will have you beheaded? Don't do it! Go away!

COMP.: We'll take that chance.

JOHN: I want to because I like the princess so much.

KING: All right. It's your head, not mine!

PRIN.: Guard! Go and get my note book at once. [*He goes and returns with the book.*] Come tomorrow morning at ten o'clock. Be ready to answer three questions.

[*John and the Companion bow and leave.*]

KING: Good. Now I can have some breakfast!

[*See 'Springboard' about bringing on the Puppet Master and his puppets at the end of Scene Three.*]

Scene Four

Place

The Palace courtyard at night.

[*The Magician appears. Monsters crawl round him. The Companion watches from behind a pillar. The Princess comes in.*]

PRINCESS: Another young man wants to marry me. What questions shall I ask him?

MAGICIAN: Will you promise to give me his eyes?

PRIN.: Yes, I will.

MAG.: Good, you must ask him what you are thinking of. Here is the first. You are thinking of your Glove. The second question—you are thinking of your Shoe. The third question—you are thinking of my head.

[*The Princess goes. The Companion kills the Magician with the rusty sword. The monsters vanish. He cuts off the Magician's head, wraps it in cloth and goes off.*]

Scene Five
Place

The Palace. *Next morning.*

KING: No, I don't feel like any breakfast to-day.

PRINCESS: What's the matter, father?

KING: What's the matter? Why, you're going to ask those silly questions again.

PRIN.: Why should that upset you?

KING: Because the young men can't answer your questions—and their heads are chopped off!

PRIN.: Good! Serves them right.

KING: Soon there won't be anyone left for you to marry.

PRIN.: I don't care. I don't want to get married.

[John and Companion come in.]

KING [*seeing them*]: Oh dear! Is it ten o'clock already?

GUARD: Yes, sir. The clock has just struck.

KING [*takes John aside and whispers*]: Go away now. Leave while your head is still on your shoulders.

JOHN: I am not afraid, sir, and the Travelling Companion will help me.

PRIN.: Are you ready?

JOHN: Yes.

PRIN.: You must guess what I am thinking now.

[The Companion whispers the answer to John.]

JOHN: You are thinking of your GLOVE!

PRIN. [*shocked*]: O-ohh!!

KING: Hurrah! What a clever fellow you are—and you really don't look it!

PRIN. [*crossly*]: What am I thinking of now?

[Companion whispers the answer to John.]

JOHN: You are thinking of your SHOE!

PRIN.: Oh! How could you know?

KING [*delighted*]: Well done, young man. [*To Princess*]: I bet you didn't expect this, did you?

PRIN. [*angrily*]: Do not think you can answer my last question so easily. What am I thinking of now?

[*Companion gives John the cloth which contains the Magician's head.*]

JOHN: You are thinking of—that!

[*The Princess screams and faints.*]

KING: How horrible! It's the head of that nasty Magician she's always going to see.

JOHN: Yes. Can I marry your daughter now?

KING: Do you want to? She may be beautiful but the Magician has made her evil.

JOHN: How can I change her?

COMP. [*gives John the three fern sticks*]: Beat her with these.

JOHN: I don't want to hurt her.

COMP.: You must drive out the evil. Beat her!

JOHN [*doubtfully*]: Well...all right. [*He gently taps the Princess with the sticks; she groans.*]

COMP.: Harder, John, harder!

[*John does so. The Princess cries out. Then John helps her up.*]

JOHN: How do you feel now, Princess?

PRIN.: Wonderful! I feel as if I've just had a lovely sleep.

KING [*dancing with delight*]: You're cured, my dear. Now I can have bacon and eggs for breakfast every day!

[*The King and Princess dance around, laughing, while everyone claps.*]

COMP.: Now you'll be happy, my friend.

JOHN: Yes, I will, thanks to you. Will you stay here with us in the Palace?

COMP.: No, I cannot. I have helped you because you helped me.

JOHN [*puzzled*]: Helped you—? When?

COMP.: Do you remember two grave-diggers? [*John nods.*]

And a man who gave all the money he had to let a dead man rest in peace ?

JOHN: Yes, I remember. But— ?

COMP.: I was the man you helped. Now my debt is paid. Good-bye. [*He vanishes.*]

JOHN: No. Don't go! Companion! [*He searches for him.*] Come back, come back.

[*He turns away sadly. The King brings his daughter to him and he begins to smile.*]

Good old Travelling Companion !

SPRINGBOARD

Group Leader:

Your group can work out a short puppet play or dance for the end of Scene Three.

A Palace Guard can announce the arrival of the Puppet Master and his puppets.

John and the Companion can stay to watch with the King and Princess.

The play or dance is performed.

Everyone is amazed because there are no strings attached to the puppets.

THE GREAT LEADER

A Play in Four Scenes

Full Cast

GUARD	HASIM
ELI	PRINCESS (Moses's foster-mother)
JOSEPH	CAPTAIN
MOSES	1ST SOLDIER
AMOS	2ND SOLDIER
MICHAEL	3RD SOLDIER
A SERVANT	AARON
PHARAOH	

Scene One

Place

A Pyramid building site.

An Egyptian guard is walking up and down watching the Hebrew slaves as they strain to move the slabs of stone. Suddenly one of the Hebrews falls down.

GUARD: Get up you lazy good-for-nothing Jew! Get up!

ELI: Water...give me water...

GUARD: Get up on your feet! You'll get water when you've done your work! [*He strikes Eli with his whip.*]

ELI: Mercy—mercy master!

[*Two of Eli's friends run over and help him up.*]

JOSEPH: Leave him alone, you bully! Can't you see he's weak with hunger?

GUARD [*cracks his whip at Joseph*]: Get back to your work— quick!

[*Joseph and his friend leave Eli and go off slowly.*]

ELI [*swaying on his feet*]: I can't...do it...I can't stand...the heat...water, water... [*he falls to the ground, accidentally ripping the Guard's tunic as he aoes so.*]

GUARD: I'll teach you to rip my tunic, you dog! [*He whips him furiously.*] Take that! and that!...and that!!

[*Moses comes in at this moment and rushes forward angrily. A spy, Hasim, is following Moses. He hides behind a rock.*]

MOSES: Why are you beating him? He's nearly dead. [*He snatches the whip from the Guard.*] Now have some of your own medicine! [*He hits him.*] See how you like it! There!

GUARD [*rushes at Moses with drawn sword*]: You traitor! He's only a Jew!

[*As he strikes at him Moses kicks up the sand, blinding him. He plunges his dagger into the Guard, killing him.*]

MOSES: What have I done? If the Pharaoh should find... [*he looks round*]. I must hide the body. [*He quickly scoops out a hole in the sand and then covers up the body.*] O Gods of Egypt, forgive me for what I have done. [*He hurries away.*]

[*The spy goes to the body and begins to uncover it.*]

Scene Two

Place

Near the Jews' Camp.

AMOS: I'll teach you to steal my bricks! [*He points to a pile of mud bricks nearby.*]

MICHAEL: I never stole your bricks!

AMOS: You thieving liar! I saw you with my own eyes.

MICHAEL: Don't you call me a thief [*he hits him*].

AMOS: You'll be sorry for that!

[*They fight and roll on the ground. Moses comes in.*]

MOSES: What are you two fighting about? Stop now!

AMOS [*getting up*]: He stole my bricks. [*He points at Michael.*]

MICHAEL: I never did.

MOSES: Stop quarrelling. Surely you need all your strength for work.

AMOS [*turning on him angrily*]: Who are you to tell us what to do?

MICHAEL: You murderer!

MOSES: WHAT?

AMOS: We know—Eli told us. He saw you kill the Egyptian guard yesterday.

MOSES: I have helped you. Now you must help me. You must not let the Pharaoh know.

MICHAEL: We will tell all to keep silent. [*They shake hands.*] You need not worry.

[*They go off towards the Jews' camp.*]

Scene Three

Place

The Pharaoh's Palace.

The Pharaoh is seated on a high throne at the far end of a great Hall. Around him are the Guards and High officials and priests from the Temple.

The foster-mother of Moses, the Princess who brought him up after he had been found in the bullrushes, is standing near the throne. She is now quite old.

A servant comes in and kneels before the Pharaoh.

SERVANT: My lord. Hasim desires an audience with you. He has come on urgent business.

PHARAOH: I will see him. [*He signals to the Guards at the door who open it and escort Hasim in.*] Bring him here. [*They come forward.*] That's far enough. Speak.

HASIM: I have information, vital information, my lord. Valuable information.

PHARAOH: Speak. You will be well rewarded.

HASIM: Yesterday I was near the Jews' Camp. And I saw one of your own Princes kill a taskmaster who was punishing a Jew.

PHARAOH [*jumps up angrily*]: What! A son of mine? Who is it?

HASIM [*nervously*]: My lord—it's—it's—

PHARAOH: Out with it, man!!

HASIM: Moses. [*There is a shocked silence.*]

PHARAOH: Moses? Impossible! You must be dreaming.

HASIM: I can show you the body—and get the Jew who was beaten, as a witness.

PHARAOH: Guards! Guards! [*They run to him.*] Go with Hasim. Bring me the body and the Jew! [*They bow and go out.*]

[*Moses's foster-mother runs forward, kneels before the Pharaoh and raises her arms, pleading to him.*]

MOTHER: O great Pharaoh, Moses would not do such a thing. He is too gentle and kind ...

PHARAOH: Yes, he *is* kind—to the Hebrews!

MOTHER [*covers her face and whispers*]: Have mercy, Great Lord, have mercy!

PHARAOH: Guards! Take this woman out and lock her in her room until we know the truth. Away!

[*She is led away crying.*]

Scene Four

Place

Somewhere in the Desert.

Moses staggers in exhausted; he crawls to a group of rocks and hides himself amongst them.

In the distance (off-stage) we can hear the voices of the Egyptian soldiers who call to each other as they search. The sounds of the search grow louder.

CAPTAIN [*off-stage*]: Hurry, you men! You'll all be behind bars if you don't find him!

1ST SOLDIER [*off-stage*]: Yes, sir.

[*The Captain comes in followed by three soldiers.*]

CAPTAIN [*pointing to soldiers*]: Now you two—search those rocks over there. [*To the other soldier*]: You can come with me. [*They go out.*]

2ND SOLDIER (*to 1st Soldier*): Come on. [*They walk towards the rocks.*] Now keep your eyes open in case the captain comes. [*They sit down on the rocks.*]

1ST SOLDIER: Phew! it's hot! [*He wipes his forehead.*]

2ND SOLDIER: I'm thirsty. [*Takes a drink from his water bottle.*] Oh, that's better! [*He places the bottle beside him on the rock. Moses reaches out from behind the soldiers, takes a drink from the bottle and replaces it.*]

1ST SOLDIER: We'll never find him around here.

2ND SOLDIER: Yes, I bet he's miles away by now. I know I would be.

[*The 1st Soldier takes a drink.*]

1ST SOLDIER: Hey! Someone's a bit greedy! [*shakes the bottle.*] You don't leave much for me, do you?

2ND SOLDIER: Who are you calling a greedy pig? I've only had a little swig.

[*Moses begins to creep away as the soldiers start to quarrel.*]

SOLDIERS [*as they argue together*]: Shut up!...I didn't!... You did!...Greedy!...Watch it, now!...Oh, yes?... Yes!...

[*As they sword-fight the Captain and 3rd Soldier come in and separate them.*]

CAPTAIN: Stop! Stop fighting, you men! What's all this fighting about?

1ST SOLDIER: We were just sitting...

2ND SOLDIER: Shut up!

CAPTAIN: What!!

87

1ST SOLDIER: I mean—he drank all the water...

CAPTAIN [*angrily*]: You're supposed to be searching for Moses!

[*Moses has now reached the furthest rock. He looks over the top. The 3rd Soldier catches sight of him.*]

3RD SOLDIER [*pointing*]: Who's that among the rocks over there?

CAPTAIN: It's Moses! Come on! [*They rush at Moses who jumps onto the rock and stands, dagger in hand, ready to fight the four men. The 3rd Soldier leaps onto the rock but before he can strike Moses stabs him and snatches up his sword.*] Now he's cornered! [*To 2nd Soldier.*] You go round to the back. [*The 2nd Soldier climbs up but falls back as Moses strikes him with his sword.*] Traitor! You'll not get away from me. [*He strikes Moses in the arm, causing him to drop his sword.*]

MOSES: You've got me now. Strike, strike now. I am ready. [*He stands waiting for the captain to strike. Aaron, Moses's brother, runs in, charges at the captain and kills him on the ground with his dagger. Moses turns to fight the 1st Soldier who runs off.*]

AARON [*gets up and goes to his brother*]: I've been searching for you everywhere.

MOSES [*laughs*]: And so have the Pharaoh's soldiers!

AARON: How's that arm of yours? [*Looks at it.*] Here, this will help. [*He tears a strip off his tunic and begins to bind the wound.*]

MOSES: How is mother? What is the Pharaoh going to do?

AARON: She's all right. But she is worried about you. What are *you* going to do? You can't come back yet.

MOSES: I know of a cave—[*he points to distant mountains*]— there is water and plenty of berries. It won't be like my old life, will it?

AARON: What are you going to do all the time you are away?

MOSES: I am going to try to find out about God—not the

God the Egyptians worship—but the God of the Jews. I shall pray for the Jews: they are treated unjustly, without mercy, and perhaps I may help them…perhaps set them free … Farewell, my brother.

[*They shake hands and Moses goes out while Aaron watches and waves farewell.*]

ALL YOUR OWN!

Now you've tried working on these plays your group can prepare one of its own.

You can take the story and the cast of one of these plays and work it out in your own way, changing anything you want to.

Write down the title and the cast.

Set out the Actions of the play, saying what the people do and what the people feel (puzzled, angry, excited and so on).

Try out your play and then improve it afterwards.

Or you can take a subject of your own.

Decide what the story is to be about.

Work out a cast for it.

Now try out the play by acting it *first*.

If it works out write down the Actions.

Then try it out again, adding anything you think it needs.

> *At the end, if you're pleased with the play you've made, you can write down the words that you have used. This is what some pupils have done, and as you have seen, some of their work has been published in this book.*